YES YES

poems

YES YES

poems

GARY GALSWORTH

CLOSE HAND PRESS
Portland, Oregon

Published by
Close Hand Press
607 NE 32nd Avenue
Portland, Oregon 97232
503-233-1784 (phone)
503-233-3091 (fax)
info@closehandpress.com (email)
www.closehandnpress.com (website)

Galsworth, Gary L.
ISBN: 1453723420

Book Design: William Stanton
Editor: Aurelia Navarro
Printed in the United States of America

Special Sales
Close Hand Press books are available at special discounts for bulk purchases.
Special editions, including personalize covers, can be created for special needs.
For more information, email us at: info@closehandpress.com

Printing Number 10 9 8 7 6 5 4 3 2 1

To my mother and to all mothers
Love's beginningless bottomless well.

And to my dear lost brother Robert
" . . . in dreams, a gentle giant rises."

This book has a muse. Without her, who knows?
The true thing is, I thought it was your
absence. It is your presence, at the end
of every thought, in everything I see.

Acknowledgments

I'd like to acknowledge the following people for their help, wisdom, encouragement, and love:

My dear friend Hanna Tierney, who simply encouraged me to take the poems I kept tripping over seriously. "Give yourself permission . . . ."

The untiring, loving support of my sister, Gwendolyn Galsworth; my loyal and talented friend and poet, Peter L. Atkinson; my former wife and friend, Janis Levine; dearest Sydney and Mik Hoffman, reader Kathryn Kimball, editor Aurelia Navarro, and book designer William Stanton.

Dear Mimi, never far from us.

And more who read, smiled, and helped: Josephine Merlino, Eva Ninoska Camilo, Justin Millan, his gutsy, angelic mom, Carol Millan, Eber Atkinson, Susan Wagner, Diane M Rubino, Robyn Somers, and last but not least Donna Marshall.

My children, Ondine and Danny: Thank you for being the part of this adventure that is most satisfying and closest to my heart.

My Zen teachers who said, *when there is nowhere else to turn, why not turn for home?*

Contents

—Three—

Branch Creek Days

and some of that glow touched us

— Four —

Words Like Taffy

what grand theater this is

— *Five* —

Bittersweet Rambles

for Yoa

— One —

In the Half Light

this mystery of promises

In the Half Light

Sitting still in the half light,
a quiet of sorts,
my mind retreats to the familiar,
working over old difficulties
conflicts without end.
The stream out back sings perfect
duets with the insects of evening.
Determined to have its way, mind
moves to a more secure position.
Stream sounds, a bit wild from
yesterday's rain,
flow through an open window
to soak me in their murmur.

Visit

I caught the slightest scent of you from across
the yard.
You standing so still, so quietly,
a small slight outline in the corner of my eye.
A shape I knew before I raised my head,
unobtrusive. No need to interrupt.
The breeze was our friend today informing our
little world of plants, birds, and hyacinths
of your arrival.
Alerted, we shared joy amongst ourselves.
The breeze then carried you up and over the
courtyard wall mingling with wisteria and such.
No need to lift my head again.
I held that small form within my heart.

Vespers

In the early hours
snow whispers past
my window

Cracking the blind
curtains of flakes give
delicious distinction
to the bare room
I stand in

Lit from Within

As if lit from within
how clearly I still see our time together.
The places, streets, curves in now familiar roads
more full of life and color than the road I'm
on now.

I hadn't seen how being with you
heightened my awareness,
focused my attention to details
and the general color of things.
Not realizing it, but there all along,
our days fairly bursting at the seams.

I keep going back to a country road
and the ribbon of coal that curved and turned
along side of it.
I can feel the mountain pressing that ribbon of coal
as we followed it back to the farm on the Rocky Branch.

Petals like Clouds

Flowers and candles
petals weightless on a darkened floor,
blue infused with lavender
they float upon these aging tiles.

The air stirred by a passerby
and petals like clouds
rearrange themselves.

When It Comes

Sometimes I like the dark. Sometimes I don't.
Today around here, with the snow melted,
branches stretching in all directions,
it's nice.

A squirrel moving along low branches in failing light,
a shadow amongst the evergreen.

When it comes, I do welcome that soft wall,
dusk into night that presses and secures
my windows.

When We Lay Close

At night,
when we lay close
she'd say, "I love you."
I can hear it, kind of shy,
reaching for me
in the dark.

After a moment, not long
long enough to think, *I want*
to say something, the right thing . . . .
I'd say, "I love you too," touching her.

And in the darkness as if
to herself, she would chuckle.
It always went like that.
Why—why that quiet laugh?
Did I say the wrong words?
What did I miss?
Everything felt fine, perfect in fact.

She'd sense something and tighten
her arms around me.

I never did figure it out—that
in between.
The man in me wondering:
What?
How do I work this?
Her man in me just welcomed
the nearness.

But tell me, really, what do
you say when the woman you
love says, all on her own,
"I love you"?

Un Homage

Did you believe hearts could break?
I did too.
I know now they don't break.
They hold the pain like
grabbing a hot fork,
hisses sears becomes
our vow of eternal love.
Inevitably we carry on,
finding refuge in the
oddest places.
Hearts scalded seared
padded footfalls
a woodcut
poignant homeless
un homage.
Hurried kisses, trembling fingers,
no safe way.
Inevitably we find refuge
in the oddest places.

Duet

tap tap tap
sounds tumble
leaf
to
leaf
rain and beech trees

Flies

At a loss I opened my mouth.
Out flew flies,
plump ones,
shapely ones too.
And flyshit and horseshit
and horses,
and a variety of drivel,
and
an insightful new angle on things.

I closed my mouth and
became a mushroom.

I'm Invisible

Look into the night
from your blanket
pitch and deep.
You'll find a window
stars looking in,
from their blanket
pitch and deep.

At Last (a visitation)

She appeared, lifted her hand and held it against my face.
Dreamlike, I pressed my face into her,
as children do to one trusted.
Then to the delight of the entire universe I was kissed,
the first of many small kisses, her lips lightly over my lips,
my face.
Tell me, what is more reassuring, more telling
than the affection in many and more
small kisses?
It happened that we became separated in distance and time
yet that sense of being and purpose lingered.
A quiet joy, a heart grateful for her finding me
once more.
Now alone again
at a loss,
how to get up, stay upright?
I did stand
and walked in stocking feet
and knew to be silent.
Words would give the lie to what had touched us.
In the silence I could still recall
our meeting place.

Last Night

Last night gave birth to icicles uncountable.
Luminous against a backdrop of endless evergreens.
Snowy curtains, chorus lines of them, bough upon bough, branch
    beyond branch.
A biting wind came, swayed and whipped great cedars,
    cascades of ice
and crusted snow rained to ground, smashing in
    crystal splashes.
Then welcome sunlight; droplets, clear yet blue,
trickle down fingers of ice and stillness.

I Share a Breath

I share a breath that shares me
and step out as worlds reach
and spines curve
in harmony.

Eyes reflect a brightness,
a curiosity cast into them,
by pointless drive-by lifetimes.

Kisses into smiles,
a shared breath,
beings in shards and splinters
find their way home.

We Become All Things

A child lifts a perfect finger.
Gently, firmly I press my fingertip to hers.
Care and affection cross this bridge between two
beings.

Time stops, worlds vanish, we become all things.
Head over heels I tumble, reaching to hold,
to capture this moment.
Say something, one word, that we may become lost in it.

Unmasked, we discover the thief of our intention,
embracing perfection, we dance a dance that cannot
be named.
Still, I am saddened by the nearness of time and change.

A child lifts her perfect finger to brush away the frown
that came between us.

Yes Yes

Rain to ice to
crystal morning.
Crystal clear inside,
crystal clear out.

Through our kitchen window
oaks covered in diamonds.
Ours for the taking.

Warm as toast we were
early morning smiles
passing back and forth,
countless smiles,
kisses beyond counting.

Our breasts compliant
in this mystery of promises.
The world beyond glazed and
crisp.

Rain to ice to crystal clear.

Two

My Journey to Date

. . . secrets, plump, richly textured

My Journey to Date

My journey to date has been largely
imaginary, both coming and going.

On the other hand there's that other—that mirror image.
My journey to date very colorful, resplendent
in paintings and gesture drawings on the inside
of my head.

By the way there's also two thumbs pressed together
exchanging the same pulse, companions against the chill.

To date, let's be frank
I'm falling behind, hopelessly behind.
I often turn to littering
for comfort and some small touch of adventure.

On the other hand, there are secrets
good ones,
richly textured, plump,
endowed with breath.

Alas, no words.
There are echoes though
and a shared pulse.

Below Ground

My friends keep slipping below ground
heading that way—the occasional stream
you follow through the woods 'til
it slips between rocks and disappears

Obviously I'm floating along with the rest
just never feels that way

Used to Fish Here

Used to fish here as a kid. Carp, sunnies . . .
"Me too," he said, "I grew up just over there,"—pointing.

He was less than half my age, but we spoke of it
as contemporaries.
"I got a four-year-old," he said, "so been coming back."

A carp broke the surface about 20 feet out.
"Not like it used to be," he said.

Really? What's changed? Having just had a conversation
with myself, walking the path around the lake, on how
it all seems so—unchanged.

Ducks honking in the weeds, bushes overhanging the water,
fireflies rising out of the grass.

What Was It Like?

It was like, there was this park
not far from my house,
and in the park was a playground.

We'd meet there once, twice
a day.

A place, a world unto itself as
our play kept creating and recreating it
catching hold of moons and stars and sliding boards.

Batman I'd say. Robin you'd say.
Johnny I'd be. Loretta you'd be.
Mars and a perfect Venus.

Playing whispering touching,
spinning and grinning for one another.
Sometimes we'd pause, look up, look around.
Was any of this happening?
Did we care?
Not really.
Not at all.

Important was, meet you here later.
The park, not far from your house,
not far from mine.

Patchito, et al.

"A concatenation of unfortunate events."
Only Patchito died of natural causes.
Fuznick, Cutie, Patchito, Meany, Willie—one by one,
they all passed into a family's history.

Yet each brought a certain illumination with it in its time,
boundless attention, and affection, though not from me.
My instincts with cats is to mistreat them,
left over from something somewhere out back, in the yard.
The care and coddling, kissing and fondling of cats,
a mother and daughter's almost fulltime passion.

The murmur of their interplay still floats around us,
to be heard again on occasion.

One by one, a lineage arose, creating joys I could not appreciate
and heartbreaks I carefully avoided, although
I did dig a hole for Patchito when he finally faded out—
even found a piece of marble cornice for his marker.

I believe it was Willie who escaped almost certain doom at
the pound by slipping into the rail yards and
weeded lots of Jersey City, placing one paw tentatively in front
 of the other, walking on eggshells, as he took those first steps
to a new life.

Holding hands, we talk about the cats and listen to the murmur
of our child's childhood.

Close and Closer

Standing to one side, moving closer, you inching back against me.
Your hip pressing my thigh, our jeans making small sounds—
closer till your hair tickles my face, your shoulder against my chest.
From the side, I press a kiss.
A smile breaks out and spreads, so close to you I know,
your whole body smiling;
reaching, turn you 'round, the marvel of it—
there you are looking up at me, a surprise to both of us
this material existence.
In grey green eyes, a most welcome easy face,
I come to rest, and it comes to mind,
didn't we have families, children, some dogs, scattered here and there?
And what of the planet, all eclipsed by a glint of moisture
in the corner of your mouth?
The world spins round us, a blur beyond your kitchen walls,
a twinkle through your kitchen window.
For you and I all movement stops
      except the movement closer.
My intention is to kiss your mouth, gently—love gently gently
can't muster it, perhaps in the future, in as long as twenty seconds or so.
Remember promising to get new kitchen cabinets for you—
      that too, soon.
All I can manage in the delight, the power of your complete presence
is to lift your hand in mine and bring each finger to my lips
the way we did our babies, when that world existed.
The very last finger kissed to the very tip, and from this
very tip
I leap into your grey green eyes and they close over me.

By Franklin's Pond

Robins hopping across a stand of swamp maples,
bare trees bumping and rubbing in the breeze,
bare trees, captured in vines and creepers.
A stark picture in charcoal and dirty browns.

But the robins are messengers of truth,
winter's done, buds to blossoms are only weeks away.

A plump green mantle will hide all this in no time.
I see furry bud tips breaking out on small branches,
robin feels the rumble of earthworms stirring.

Chivalry Revived

It came to me recently (coming through the
Lincoln Tunnel) that I had had no choice
but to punch Lewis Goldman,
my best friend at the time, hard in the stomach.

Sorry, I have no recollection
of what he did wrong
or what he said that was
not allowed.

I am clear it was unpardonable
and my duty was to punch him,
sucker punch him, hard as I could.
And that's what happened.

Issues

I had issues, he said, issues with my father.
I thought wow, simple. He and his Dad had issues.
Pop just beat the shit out of me.
Though not as often as it seemed at the time,
from the perspective of a rabbit trapped on the stairs,
about to be crushed, extinguished.

Yeah, I got beat, and everything considered
not unnecessarily, except in my quick young eyes.
In spite of appearances, wherein Mr. Wade,
the local cop, threatened his arrest,
Pop was full of concern and fear for my
inner and outer well being.

Sensing the rhythms of time and circumstance
as I got older, kept a door, or other means of escape,
between him and me. When the air turned electric,
when the room gained a certain crispness
and sparkle, only location and reflexes mattered.
At an early age I developed an instinct for predators,
for impending violence, especially disguised as disinterest.

I could read the air turning up its charge of protons,
could sense the inevitability—someone's going to get eaten today—
someone who is not quick, quick as can be.

In grown-up life, this sense of critical mass
would cause me to dissolve into action, strike first,
resulting in bloody but positive outcomes, against the odds.
The bigger the better.

Screwy as it sounds, I had a secret belief that Pop was choreographing
all these threats and cul-de-sacs, these seemingly random
emergencies, to prepare for and insure my survival
in the real coming emergency: Life.

Issues? I had no issues with my father. Nothing that indirect,
nothing that remote. He called me *mamela* when I was little.
"Mother's love" in Yiddish or Italian. A tenderness in the words
as he spoke them. I grew with a sense of being attended to,
cared for, unprohibited—knew fear of him but little else.

He was full of stories about storms at sea and violence on land,
of Buffalo Bill in Switzerland, and starving Russians and their resolve.
Of Jews, Italians, and real Americans. Of how things worked and why
they wouldn't, of friends and loyalty in the crunch, and how
to use a hidden razor if you had to. A cycle of stories I'd ask to hear
over and over again, knowing all the good parts by heart.
The good parts, the good days, and the tough days.
Tough moments really, as the earth was solid beneath my feet.
More so for me than for him.

He knew a lot, took too much personally. It was in part his torment.
His shouts of rage, of frustration, that sometimes bled to howls
of pain and self-blame. Nevertheless, my father had a full heart
and a loving heart, but a heart that was somehow broken.

See-Saw

Paper towel eater paper towel
eater—eater
used to can her beans green
about so long—plenty salt
used to rock her babies down to sleep
worked and nursed "their souls to keep"
lined her young ones in tobacco
rows cut down hoes

marched 'em shooed her young ones
down the rows
their father plowing on up the hill
his tired smile her strength her will
paper towel eater—young
ones gone or turned to stone or
turned to heart gone to our lord
to church suppers places where the land's
flat the road's straighter

mischief in a crooked smile
she says "Can you do this? I guess you can't . . ."
glancing down to bare feet and all those toes
two big ones crossed over two small ones—that
ol' schoolyard trick
little girl from the hills finally gets to play

About See-Saw

I met Opal Allen a few years ago.

Once during a conversation I commented on how hard farm families had to work in eastern Kentucky back then. She said, " . . . well, we don't have a way of thinking of hard work or not hard work. If it needs to be done, we do it. That's how it is."

Opal met her husband when she was 12 and married him at 16 years old. She spent her whole busy life on their hill farm on the Rocky Branch (they had some good flatland for tobacco, down along the river), raised a large family, kept everyone alive and clean in spite of the odds, and saw that all the kids went to college.

And she remained forever in love with her "good man." Opal "caught the Alzheimer's" shortly before I met her and by her mid 80's was not connecting the dots too well. Her decline was setting in.

There's a lot to say about Opal Allen, but I'll leave it at—I'm glad to have met her and got to know her a bit. (She would show her daughter Mary and I her precious and wonderful quilts again and again.) The previous poem, "See-Saw," is during her decline.

G.L.G.
Lexington, Kentucky
November, 2007

A Miracle of Sorts

Bends and curves, you'd call it a back road.
Folks that use it see a main road.
The center of the mountains in the center
of south eastern Kentucky
There's new black-top now, still few guard rails.

At the side of this road, near the curve to the
Rocky Branch, there's an overgrown place.
Brambles, bushes, small trees, and, if you look
twice, you'll see inside this nest a small wooden
building. More a large shed.
Clapboard siding, galvanized roof, all akimbo
and falling in.
Can you make out that rusted sign, still nailed up,
for your favorite soda pop.

Then it was bright with fresh browns and reds,
and called to a little girl in a homemade dress,
holding her dad's calloused hand. Hers held in his,
not so unlike the vines and plants nesting an old
important place.
A place glanced at now and then by—once upon
a sunny day—passersby.

She can still taste a licorice, a cherry soda pop,
see an exotic and perfect future held in the small
corner rack of magazines.
Listen to voices coming off big familiar shapes,
that were met there, grinned at, open faced.

Hear her father's resonant voice permeate the air around her, a protective vigilant, while she decided on how to spend the silver dime, held tightly at the very bottom of her pocket. Quietly engrossed in the limitless prospects of this great mountain oasis.

A miracle of sorts, was it not.

Drive-in

odd how thoughts unfold into stories in a blink
there it is
a chain of events projected onto the inside of our
skulls from the projection-booth fold in our
brains
seen recognized contexted by that far seeing internal
eye
looking out from another brain fold
to then be infused with atmosphere warmth and
intent by a heart link fold—wired right down our neck
to ventricles enthusiastically delivering messages
of interest
that odd looping relay of never ending hand-offs moving
at best to a place of seemliness and regularity as each
foot rises and falls
from another fold—the "appearance of actually
being there" fold—we stand back and appraise
all this activity
judge and sort
come to terms find momentary relief settling into
the days first life saving cup of coffee just as the
projector starts blinking and we are handed off
not a beat missed to the next twinkling celluloid
episode

Purple Blessing

A failed experiment in coloring you'd say,
oh boy, your purple hair stage
and we'd laugh.

It was a favorite time, a time of blossoming,
of purple flowers, of discovery—discovering you,
behind the shower curtain, your smile and welcome
radiating like sunshine—discovering an unexpected sense
of completeness being near this purple-haired woman.
My appetite for you edged out all else. "Hungry?" you asked.
Not really. —"What shall we do ?"—Doesn't matter.
Being a worker, "a farm girl," as you'd say, you boiled some eggs
and we laughed.

Nothing was ugly, everything was random and perfect, patterns
still unformed, discovering fear could be held at bay,
by this color—ours.

Discovering you again and again in a tangle of sheets, finding
the smooth of your neck in a tangle of hair, the perfection there—
and we laughed.

With time, tears came and made the colors run, stained your
cheeks and mine, shadows bled into the wonderment.
Now I walk a pink and clay red landscape,
full of canyons, a bubbling stream, cool and fresh to be near.
Ahead a desert flower bright with spring and welcoming,
in a color we'd know as ours
and we'd smile.

— *Three* —

Branch Creek Days

. . . and some of that glow touched us

Branch Creek Days

I.

Night snowed to first light
looking up
everything is white
just yesterday I too changed shirts

II.

It's happening
it's happening
everything that can
is turning green
the browns and grays
of yesterday
are dressed in spring

III.

Big tree
broke off in a storm
still points a jagged finger
at threatening skies

IV.

October shadows
spotted dog
turns lawn chair
in the twilight
what havoc will be
wrought after dark

Sitting

Sitting face to the sun
made a chilly day snug.
The mountain rose
the sun went down
a chill crept into my clothes,
and sunshine turned
a dimming afternoon.
The wind came
charged my door like a lion.
Always the artful partner I
stood up and bowed.

Fallen from the Nest

Today, hard news on the bottom step.
An unwelcome sight
the hardest of facts.

Compounded in knowing that this
was beyond my hands to touch,
to interfere.

Fallen from the nest.
I wanted to interfere, do something,
amend it, call a power on high—please . . .

All I could do was fall in with the slow
regular breathing, the naked rise and fall,
and keep myself from staying too long.

Red Mesa

The sun drops behind that
big red mesa
taking a winter's day with it

snow melt runs in rivulets
from shadow to shadow

Guilty Global Warming

Every time our eyes met
ear to ear smiles were born.

Every time I saw you, near or far,
or you me,
a smile was born.

How many millions of smiles did
we bring into the world
during our time?

Enough for climate change perhaps.

Late

There's a dove on the power
line that runs by the house

further down there was a whole
line of blackbirds—swaying together

only two are left
with a wide gap between them

sunset seems to call birds to
it
the dove stays
to coax the shadows from the trees

Can't Answer

He had tears in his eyes
walking past
I don't know I started crying too

but it wasn't much of a stretch
I suppose the well of tears is as close
as the well of joy

reminds me of raining—stepping into
a puddle wearing that pair of shoes
with worn soles

Winter's Passing

A patch of old melting snow spreads across
the mossy ground.
How tenderly I love you.
A brown leaf, left with the passing of
far away autumn, lies motionless before me.
The loveliness of your black hair teases
the memory in my fingers.
Vines, now brown and crisp with winter's passing,
clutch the pilasters between each arch and give
this place the feeling of a cloister in medieval times.
The beauty and innocence of your face, the passion
that rests quietly in your eyes, warms me
and clouds my thoughts.
Tree limbs pierce the grey uninviting sky in a thousand
places, and the air is permeated with the feeling of
transition.
Spring will feel good against me and against the
growing belly of my beloved.

Cat Bones

Cat bones, my bones, share
the same old bag.
The same sinews tie and
work us.

Resting against each other
out of the sun,
bound by daydreams, and
half closed eyes.

It's Spring

It's spring
and cottonwoods reach
to drink the moon
as it drifts across a hundred ponds

Who's Going to Look after Opal?

I.

Mimi, leaning forward in her wheelchair,
hands gripping the arm rests.
Chin forward like a sign post—directions to the
nursing station.
Down the corridor I see her talking.
There is an urgency, a purpose in her movements.
"My medication?
and when will Mario be back?
can I lie down now—
why not?
my parents, what of my parents,
are they here?
nurse—nurse—they live here
They are here, I'm sure."
Lost teeth give new angles to her face
as she looks up at me.
"No Mim, I am not your mother,
perhaps I should have been."
(could I then take you away from here?)
There is a softness, a yielding,
in her brown eyes.
What have I promised that she looks at me like that?

Isadora, long scarves
wrap around the flare of her hips.
Is she really gone without a trace?

II.

"Mary, where's Mary?"
Opal at the far end of the dining hall,
her new pink sweater and pants, a size too large.
Her hair washed and brushed.
Turning slowly, looking across the room.
Not frightened, just a little anxious, a little concerned.
It's her trust that keeps the world she inhabits from
cracking and becoming the wilderness that awaits.
"Mary, where's Mary?"

Looking out the kitchen window,
past the garden, she'd see deer
and wild turkey,
and—the irrepressible percolations of children,
tribes of them.

III.

They trusted us.
And so when it was time,
we led them
held out our hands to them,
and they, childlike, took hold.
Trusting us, we led them to their death.
It came down to us.
No one else would take them, had the capacity,
the innocence to love them so completely,
the lambs.
It's not reconcilable,
nor should it have been otherwise.
This journey, with its myriad activities, its varieties,

the occasional wail of sirens.
But isn't that asking a bit too much of love?
I guess not. I guess love is that,
is that too.
I guess it's big enough to carry us,
and what we now know,
but I'm not sure.

Looking back at burning cities,
the Old Testament's warning
on questioning that which is ours to do,
but not ours to turn or twist or tinker with.

Crickets

Crickets sawing away
in every bush and thicket.
A song to dusk, who
bows ever more deeply.

As to myself and mine, we're
doing all we can
to keep the sun from setting.

In my heart of hearts, I'm
on the side of the crickets.

View from Two Boys

As usual, I thought I could start a dialogue,
"cherry pop or lemon ice?"
He took a cup of plain water and drank it back.
  Optimistic, I thought I could be in dialogue with him.
"A little help on this," I said. Instantly he took off running,
leaving me with socks dangling from my fingers.
  Ran up over Red Hill, across the old golf course
(abandoned these many years) through the brambles
to the top of Cemetery Hill.
  I could just see him past the oaks and maples
near that stand of birch.
  I waved. Banking on the power of resurrection and
recollection, I thought I could start a reminiscence with him.
"Remember when we rode our bikes down Cemetery
Hill, always too steep. You smashed into that thicket, got
all scratched up, broke your balls on the crossbar!"
  He abandoned me at the scene of the accident.
I found him beyond the crest among the headstones.
  "Sure has grown over the years, this field of marble."
He reads, "Amos Young , born 1932, died 1955."
  "Golly not very old," I said. He moved on to another
stone.
  Due to an excessive chin (they called me *hog jaw* in
the service), I thought now was a good opportunity.
  We pee'd against the trunk of a maple tree, I intent
on making ants run for cover.
  He allowed a long sigh, the sun glinting off his yellow
cascade.

I wondered if this was like nourishment for a tree. "Do you think this helps the tree grow?"

"Watch, you're about to step in it," he said and turned away.

Every Raindrop

Tires cut a swath through
the soaked roadway.
Instantly water starts
softening the edges, filling back.

Yesterday there was a great banquet
of snow here.
Today every raindrop swallows
some of it.

Friction

Friction of an exquisite sort
waves lapping the
shore

Rain Buds

A pasture near that big red barn
where we passed a calf
just as it got born.
The farmer, in black knee boots,
struggling through a wet meadow.
His two dogs, bounding, and yelping.
The boots were a chore to move fast in.
He trying to reach the newborn
before the dogs, excited as hell, did any mischief.
A drizzly, drizzly day it was.
The road slick.
We pulled over to maybe help
and watch.
I can feel the rain on my face and eyelashes
and see your hair covered in rain buds.
We stood on the road,
in some wonder, and some worry.
The calf didn't even know she was born—
a yellow glow came off her.
Some of that glow touched us
and though we felt as wanderers,
hand in hand, it was you
who brought me to such unlikely places.
And it left me quietly beholden.

(for Mara)

—Four—

Words Like Taffy

what grand theater this is

Words Like Taffy

Pulling words like taffy
folding them together
finding interesting momentums
after a third cup of coffee
watching friends and outsiders carry
off the ticking minutes
listening to the sound the song
of a life
of its resilience
sound and song
and words
folding them together
one into the other
like taffy

Oriental

She'd been sitting there, hands
clasped in her lap, for what seemed
a long while.
Then she raised her hands and arms.
My eyes moved with them.
She brought her hands together
as if in prayer. Gently rubbing finger
tips and palms together.
A comforting play. Affirming.
The warmth of interest moved in me.
As with half closed eyes
I followed along till suddenly she
dropped her pale hands into the folds
of her skirt
and was still again.

Gentler, Kinder

In order to stay with us she
had to start breathing.
My breath became hers, our lips met,
pressed and, for the fleetest moment,
were together again in this harlequin story.
It didn't play out; a love greater than mine
was reaching for her,
a lover gentler, much sweeter than I embracing her.
Gone, I tried to let her go, washing away
with tears and sobs some of my difficulties.
We went our separate ways,
mine still bound, seeking freedom, passage;
hers beyond the reach of a story's bondage.
My breath it is hers, still and always,
she brushes my cheek in even the smallest
whisper;
mine finds hers, she breathes me in every exhalation.

Your Absolute Stillness

Your absolute stillness
my still speaking heart
kindness before the birth
of words
your hand held in mine
are we not lingering

life and death with
nowhere to go

Dawn

Dawn filters through candle light
flowers in a simple vase
the bright tip of an incense stick
burns down imperceptibly
no monk sits next to it
his absence fills the place
it breathes
and accommodates my passage

I Will

I'm not ready.
> *Ready..?*

I'm going, soon, I know that.
> *Where you going?*

That's it. I can't stand that. I don't
know, and you can't tell me!
> *I hope I know better than to try.*

Thanks for coming, but you're
no help.
> *Don't ask me to leave.*
> *More than anything, I'd like to*
> *help.*

I'm not ready; and what about
those, all those that have already
gone?
> *Where?*

I feel their loss, but it doesn't
bring one over—can we stay
close just now, keep talking,
whisper?
> *I will.*

Lean over here—whisper to me.

(for Laurie)

Dream

Dream within dream
our bubble arising
we vanish in the "pop"

When It's Time

You don't give up, you
don't give up,
and then there comes the time
when it's time to give up.

Have you seen that in people?
They keep on going,
keep on,
and then the moment comes;
a kid's balloon rising over the park,
heading for the far away, and
from the inside out—you let it go.

Bathed in Sunlight

This afternoon I had a guest
we bathed in sunlight
later shadows fell across
the room
and night became our host

Don't Go

Living with her ghost for so long
moving between tormented memory
and tearfully joyous reverie
admittedly I did beg for relief
face in hands sinking into love's well
that beginningless bottomless
well

Her ghost—becoming more transparent
vaporous
starting to blend in the mists
that descend with spring mornings
I know even her ghost is little by little
leaving

My heart should feel some touch of
relief
some sense of coming day and light
but all it says is
don't go don't go

Not Raining

It's not raining, it's not snowing,
it's quiet, there are no people on the street.
Through the overcast, a steeple barely visible;
on nearby roofs, wisps of smoke drift and diffuse. The
parking lot below, its black surface already wet.

There are few cars, the early birds now on a ferry
to New York.

It's chilly on the water. Grateful fingers
press a warm cup of coffee,
as the boat shudders and shoulders
its way toward an invisible city.

Anniversary

For months I planned, anticipating
the letter I'd write, on the six-month
anniversary of your "change of mind."

And so it came to pass
that that letter was written.
Many times.
As I commuted or sat in quiet places
(and noisy places) with a coffee.

Pecked out, edited,
and after some sighs,
some tears, some secrets,
mailed.

I waited. No flag went up,
no drawbridge was lowered,
no dent was made.

A determined sort with a lively
but limited fantasy life
akin to the appetite of my good-natured
but easily confounded dog,
I anticipated the letter I'd write
on the nine-month anniversary of
your looking back, to wave
and smile and drive away.

Mimi

the noise of passage stilled
a door stops swinging
days decades an infinity of seasons
call back for order recognition
then silence that perfect offering
enfolds us
our hearts open
and we are together again

Love in the Park

Walking talking about time
its elasticity its tyranny
how one's vertebrae get brittle grow bony spurs and
the large crop of rabbits this spring
on the knoll ahead
people clustered around telescopes
looking at moons
clustered around giants
all held in time
limiting even the hugeness of Jupiter
I listen to the lilt in your voice
a dialect all its own
the origins of song—the rings of Saturn
far from the reach of stiffening time

Inocente

Originally the screen
was blank the house dark
the audience still looking
for parking

then
in silhouette
an old couple hand in hand
and with every step
they disappear into each other

what grand theater this is

—*Five*—

Bittersweet Rambles
for Yoa

Some of the Things

Some of the things I'll do when
we do this again
Sit on the same side of the table in
restaurants
I loved sitting across to look
into your eyes
watch the animation of your face
and smiles but I'd trade that off to let our thighs touch
arms rub
let your hair get in my way

Touching as much as possible and beyond
unseemly so
erase the boundary of where I end and
where we begin
be more openly affectionate with small
caresses to your arms the back of your hands my fingers
trailing over yours
more friendly kissy be a pest with kisses
your cheek your forehead
passions complement

And when you came into our room naked
which in our familiarity was often and always a delight
delight in touching you each time
hands and palms over hips small of back
overcome the pleasure of the vision to stand close
just short of passion—
when we lay in bed

which was often of two overtired people
be sure to flip around put my head
to your feet nibble your toes
always at least do that before the long day's end
fall asleep in your laughter

And should you become fat again
make you squash me like you used to
we'd find a way to both love that moment
maybe I could convince you to simply kill me
in the loveliness—being squashed by you

And of course everything we do will
as it was
be done over and over and over for the first time

Charlie's Funeral

looking out the window
there is just sky

and the branch of a tall
slash pine reaching
across it

the branch ends in long
green needles that shimmer
as the light passes through them

My Friends

Do you have friends here ?
>   *"Mario, he has affection for me.*
>   *And the girl who's been on Depicol for five years.*
>   *Very crazy, but nice."*

I see.
In luminous bits and pieces
the moon rises through the trees behind us.
>   *"The man with cats, all his brothers are alcoholics.*
>   *He gave me my new book.*
>   *The other place people tormented me with Jesus.*
>   *Doctor was ignorant and always droopy—dopey and droopy."*

How's the doctor here?
>   *"I don't know. I've found my higher power,*
>   *the trees, the moon.*
>   *Last night it was round and full.*
>   *I spend my time there, finding serenity."*

Ah yeah, it's behind the building.
>   *"I love that building, but the people,*
>   *nasty, crazy.*
>   *The wheelchair people, they run over your foot, on purpose.*
>   *And the dreams, a disturbing place."*

What about your novela ?
>   *"Can't look at TV, with these old women talking their heads off,*
>   *in their own worlds.*
>   *But I'm all right, in fact, I'm happy.*
>   *See how shiny and round the moon is?*
>   *I see it as my friend."*

Simulated Life

Sitting on the edge of the bed on the phone
with an old friend
talkin' about this and that—a voice inside
cries: *I want to go home*
eyes get damp and that's enough
but who is it that wants so badly to go home
and where is home anyway

It's not this hotel room is it smelling of cigarettes
windows you break your fingers to crack open
danish and coffee—Continental Breakfast served
in a cardboard box in the lounge

On the sidewalk—are we all walking to the bus stop
doesn't that fellow look like he's asking himself the
same question hearing the same voice inside
then opening my notebook for instructions at an outdoor table
    get a hat—wide brimmed—straw   *go to ATM*
    call Jo after 2—thank her

Sliding off the bench
tucking instructions and glasses away
rough concrete scrapes the bottom of
my shoes
soles and sidewalk find each other like a gritty handshake

Claire de Lune (exile, desolation, devastation)

I.

Claire de Lune! Claire de Lune! I shout.
What's that smell and where's it going?

My dick used to be incredibly hard.
Tight dick, tight thoughts, clarity in cognition one
could call it; or maybe just clearly narrow minded.
I could pee across the yard if need be, across the
wood pile and hit the dog rooting around on
the other side.

Things have become more stringy of late, kind
of stringy of late.
Like there's more air leaking through my brain,
but not in a bad way. It's more a breeze than
a draft.
Nevertheless, the question remains, did I create
this, or just get lost in it?
A well meaning breeze gone west.

II.

Smells like . . . burnt toast!
Can you picture it? Ma would scrape the char off.
A layer of black flecks dusting the garbage. The
remains, a toast failure. White bread, always
a fragile thing, tasty but fragile.

III.

On occasion I was cruel to my mother.
She would start cooking the spaghetti too early.
Then serve it with determination,
apprehension,
and a certain joyful eagerness.
The meatballs were always good, heavy,
but good—*Claire de Lune! Claire de Lune!*
I'd yell.
Al dente! Al dente! would echo around
the room. That sorry plate of spaghetti. Ma
would sag a little more.

Go! Stomp around the yard. Let cold air and
cold stars dissolve the mystery of it and comfort
thee!

The kid, poised with knife and fork over his
plate, hungry but nervous. Awaiting the go ahead
from someone who knew . . . , safe to eat yet?
Seeing him, Ma felt okay again.
"Eat, it's fine. Your father is tired and works
hard." Resigned, forgiving, and busy attending
the youngster.
Was there a problem here?
Ask her.

This Little Mystery

Jo said, "They remind me of a group of
old friends. You know what I mean?
See some are doing poorly, wilting
and others look just fine; don't seem to have aged
at all."
I looked at the yellow roses gotten a few days ago
arranged in a blue vase, in those various states of
being, from still full and robust, to bent and showing
the onset of decay.
Next stop a garbage bag.
She's right. Shaking my head, looking them over.
How full of life they all were on making their
acquaintance recently.
This little mystery served with breakfast.

An Endless Presence

My mother, it was my mother,
who stood between me and eternity.
Comfort. An endless presence,
till she slipped quietly over
the edge.

Epicenter

Teeth. These teeth are changing. Time moving so fast,
I can feel the wear, the texture of it.
Am I losing it here, outside my mouth, the me outside my mouth?
Can't answer that 'cause if I were, I'd be the last to know.
There are some people that do know, can see, but can't speak of it.
If you've been with crazy people, you understand, they are the last to
know. They think it's happening.
We're telling them, and anyone else who will listen, it's not.
Wrestling them to the ground in defense of what's not happening.
They're telling us it's a complete mistake and we are in complete
agreement. Tearing the knees out of good slacks, in the face of this
huge mistake; scraping knuckles and knees on rough floors
as we drive another crazy into submission.
Time moving so fast, I can feel the wear, the texture of it.

9-Fingered Poem

He keeps falling in love with women whose mothers,
ghosts with mailed fists,
rise up out of graveyards and wheelchairs
to intercede.
The girls, recognizing the shape and scent of their
Amazon adversaries,
are quick to react.
Donning helm and Kevlar vest, they grab
their great shield by his arms and legs,
and rush to the attack.

Janis and a Thoughtful Man.

Bill moved steel.
When you drive across the GW Bridge, and you're
looking up at the silver immensity of it, your mind gets
caught in the steel.
Girders, webbing, cables, an infinity of pieces, riveted and
bound by more steel.
Well—Bill shipped all of it. In his ordered, organized,
and quiet way, he delivered that bridge.

He had, in life, another more personal bridge; a bridge from
working, planning, and control to variety, stimulation,
and naïve discovery of oneself. That bridge, Milly, his wife.
Bill would start his day, and his day with her,
long before breakfast. Picking up the newspapers outside their
apartment door, he'd carry them to a chair by the big window.
And read them front to back.

One day, in his robe, he sat down and could not read.
His eyes failing, could no longer make the words.
That afternoon, when he took off his robe and went to bed,
he didn't get out of it again.

In time, he had himself shipped to a nursing home.
His room overlooked the steel mill and mill stacks
Once a valley filled with activity, filled with haze and smoke
and the flickering glow of furnaces.
Now the air was clear and chill, the picture was a quiet one of
great rusted buildings. All empty.

Smokeless silent stacks, improbably tall and indestructible.

A million cold bricks.

Nevertheless, they were comfortably, even serenely familiar, to a man who used to move the steel out of them.

On a day, Janis, in her tan winter coat, came to visit.
Janis and her good friend Milly joined in the timeless and limitless adventure of Tea—*chanoyu*.
Moving quietly, with gentle precision in the activity of bowing and kneeling and lifting small objects.
The choreography of Tea. Their respective identities absorbed in harmony and interplay.
How different was it from building a colossal perfect bridge ?

Bill asleep, Janis stood watching. He opened his eyes and found her, took in her presence.
His arm came up and, with a thin crooked finger and the movement of his hand, called her over.
Gentle, ever respectful, she didn't move.
Bill repeated the gesture, his thin finger insistent.
She came close, put her face close to his. His breathing, not deep, and laboring a little. Hers, steady, almost inaudible.
After a time together, Bill said, " Goodbye, Janis."

A kind and thoughtful man.

Pink Edges

It's finally stopped raining and some yard work is getting done.
The hedges have gotten way ahead of themselves,
so cutting them back's the place to start.
With all the rain, it's Amazonia here this spring.

Half way along the hedgerow that runs the front of our property,
is a rose bush. In full bloom now, some petals lying here and there
on the ivy ground cover.

White roses. Not white white, but softer.
A cream white with pink edges.

Cutting and trimming, coming up to them carefully so's not to
disturb the blossoms.
The smell of roses, you can almost taste it.
Pop planted these, and I'm reminded of him.

In his travels, such a while ago, he snipped some cuttings
and planted them up by the porch and in the middle of these hedges.
They've been making flowers and blossoms for all these years.
"I got them," he said, "because your mother has a love for roses."

Growing up here things were, in their way, pretty solid yet also
touch and go. Very much that way.
Not far from the ocean, not far from the woods.
The old abandoned golf course and red hill.
Time was, I'd drink a whole quart of milk,
when I got home from school.

There was also crying, yelling, some violence. Even when
it wasn't there, which was most of the time, it was there.

I was about 11 years old when Pop put in the roses, and told me
of Mom's love for them.
Privately, silently, I was taken aback. I saw he had
a connection to Mom; he liked her.

And that it was more original, at least as true, as the
terrible scenes I believed were them.

A first sense that the wreckage littering my world
was not what it seemed.
That there were sanctuaries.

Auras

There may exist angels, warrior angels,
that go head to head with demons.
The angels I've known don't do that.
They persist, and sometimes prevail, by
simply getting back on their feet, without
anger or remorse, and attending.
Brushing the scuffs off white
auras, they, with a homey elegance,
continue to arrange things in the
appropriate way.

And ride the beast pressing into them,
enveloping it in joys unfettered by eternity.

Like Clouds

thoughts crowd me like clouds
round that mountain over there
rains come and gone
just an occasional drop working
its way off the roof

hoping for more
the welcome in rain sounds

we had these moments
filled overflowing whole days even
coffee conversations listening
interested

a look a thought shared sweets
two mushrooms growing in our own
shadowed corner of the yard
nudging and leaning into each other

of You

eyes closing I think of
you
when they open I think
of you
and in between we
are together

About the Author

Gary Galsworth was born and grew up in the New York City area. After high school, he spent three years in the Marine Corps before attending the Art Institute of Chicago and the University of Chicago, majoring in painting and, later, filmmaking. He made a number of films during the late 60s into the 70s.

Gary is a plumber and a student of Zen, practicing with his 103-year-old teacher, Joshu Sasaki Roshi, since 1976. Poetry began as a quiet aside. The oldest poem in this collection, "Winter's Passing," is from 1964.

His daughter, Ondine, is a mom, yoga instructor, and writer; and his son, Danny, is a banjo-playing cyclist who goes to school in Los Angeles.

Gary lives in Hoboken, New Jersey, spends a good part of his time in an old house in Long Branch on the Jersey Shore, and travels regularly to New Mexico and California.

You may contact Gary directly at his email: gdplumber@aol.com

Made in the USA
Charleston, SC
15 June 2014